THE OLYM

CRISES AT THE OLYMPICS

HAYDN MIDDLETON

The Olympic spirit

The modern Olympic Games began in 1896. Since then the Games' organizers have tried to ensure that every competitor keeps to the true Olympic spirit. This spirit is based on fair play, international friendship, a love of sport purely for its own sake and the ideal that it is more important to take part than to win.

Heinemann
LIBRARY

First published in Great Britain by Heinemann Library,
Halley Court, Jordan Hill, Oxford OX2 8EJ,
a division of Reed Educational and Professional Publishing Ltd.
Heinemann is a registered trademark of Reed Educational & Professional Publishing Limited.

OXFORD MELBOURNE AUCKLAND
JOHANNESBURG BLANTYRE GABORONE
IBADAN PORTSMOUTH NH (USA) CHICAGO

Designed by AMR
Originated by Dot Gradations
Printed in Hong Kong/China

04 03 02 01 00
10 9 8 7 6 5 4 3 2 1

ISBN 0 431 05926 8
This title is also available in a hardback library edition (ISBN 0 431 05921 7)

British Library Cataloguing in Publication Data
Middleton, Haydn
  Crises at the olympics. – (The olympics)
  1.Olympic games (Ancient) – Juvenile literature 2.Olympics
  Political aspects – Juvenile literature
  I.Title
  796.4·8

Acknowledgements
The Publishers would like to thank the following for permission to reproduce photographs:
Allsport: pp6, 7, 8, 10, 12, 13, 15, 19, 24, 25, 26, 27, 28, 29, IOC Olympic Museum p4, Pressens
Bild p5; Associated Sports Photography: pp17, 20; Colorsport: pp16, 18, 21; Corbis/Bettmann:
p14; Kobal Collection: Warner Brothers Pictures p11; Popperfoto: p22; Sporting Pictures (UK)
Ltd: p23.

Cover photograph reproduced with permission of AP File.

Every effort has been made to contact copyright holders of any material reproduced in this
book. Any omissions will be rectified in subsequent printings if notice is given to the Publisher.

For more information about Heinemann Library books, or to order, please phone
++44 (0)1865 888066, or send a fax to ++44 (0)1865 314091. You can visit our website
at www.heinemann.co.uk.

Any words appearing in the text in bold, **like this**, are explained in the Glossary.

Contents

Introduction

The modern Olympic Games began in 1896. With breaks during World Wars One and Two, they have been held at four-yearly intervals ever since. The first Games were staged in Greece, home of the Olympics in ancient times. The next scheduled Games will be held in Sydney, Australia, in the year 2000.

The 1996 organizers called their Games – in Atlanta, USA – 'the largest peacetime social event in human history'. It would be hard to argue with that. From small beginnings in 1896, the Games have become a wonderful celebration not just of international sport but also of healthy competition.

Tarnish on the gold

Over the years, however, these peaceful Games have featured a high number of incidents, controversies, scandals and even tragedies. In this book you can read about some of them. They range from the appalling organization of the 1900 Games in Paris, to the outrage caused at Seoul in 1988 when 'the Fastest Man on Earth' tested positive for drugs after winning the 100 metres gold medal.

Adolf Hitler watches over the opening of the 1936 Olympic Games in Berlin, Germany.

As you will see, many problems have arisen when Olympic sport has become mixed up with politics. Some people say that sport and politics are completely separate and should always stay that way. But as the Games grew bigger, and more and more people took an interest in them through the **media**, governments realized that they could use the Olympics to score political points over their rivals and enemies.

No one knew this better than Adolf Hitler, whose **Nazi** Party ruled Germany when the Games were held in its capital city, Berlin, in 1936. Hitler planned to turn the Olympics into a showcase for the all-round supremacy of the German people. On pages 12 and 13 you can see what became of this early attempt to **pervert** the true 'Olympic spirit'.

Political rivalry at the Games became especially open and bitter from 1952 onwards. The USA and **USSR**, global superpowers, seemed to be conducting a kind of peacetime warfare through their athletes. Their rivalry grew until, in 1980, the USA refused to send a team to the Olympic Games in the USSR. Then, in 1984, the USSR stayed away from the Los Angeles Games in the USA. You can read about these unfortunate **boycotts** on pages 22 and 23.

Problems in perspective

Perhaps we should not be surprised that there have been so many Olympic crises. Any event that brings together competitors from so many nations (197 in Atlanta) is bound to have problems. The dream of Olympic glory drives men and women from all over the world to great heights of achievement. The same dream has also been behind most of the stories that follow....

You can find out what Olympic outrage this **terrorist** was involved in on pages 16 and 17.

Is this the Olympic Games?

Nowadays when the Olympic Games are on, TV, radio and newspapers make sure that people all over the world know about what is happening. But the first three Games of the modern era – at Athens in 1896, at Paris in 1900 and at St Louis, USA, in 1904 – were not so well publicized. Plenty of people remained blissfully ignorant that these Games were being staged. In fact, even some *competitors* were unaware that they were involved in the Olympics. Good organization was not a feature of the modern Games' early history!

Farce in France

Compared to what followed in 1900 and 1904, the 1896 Games in Athens were a miracle of efficiency. The quality of the sport was often low, but the large crowds had a wonderful time – and afterwards many Greeks thought that the four-yearly Games should always be held in their country. But Baron de Coubertin, the 'Father' of the modern Olympic Movement, had an *international* vision – and the second Games were scheduled to take place in Paris, capital city of France, his own home country, in 1900.

A poster for the 1900 Games in Paris, which were part of a much larger fair. Facilities for the athletes were very poor and public interest was very low.

This turned out to be a bad idea. That year, a great fair called the Universal Exposition was also being held in Paris. The Games – strung out from May to October – turned out to be little more than a sideshow within it. Spectators were few and far between, facilities and officials were often of a poor standard and very few people seemed to know quite what was going on. American Margaret Abbott won the women's golf 'because', she later explained, 'all the French girls apparently misunderstood the nature of the game scheduled for that day and turned up to play in high heels and tight skirts'.

When these Games limped to an end, even de Coubertin had to admit: 'We have made a hash of our work.' He could only hope that the next Olympics – to be held across the Atlantic Ocean in St Louis in 1904 – would be a big improvement. But maybe he guessed they would not be, because he did not even travel all the way there himself – nor did many foreign competitors.

Absurdity in America

The 1904 Games were held as part of the World's Fair. Again events were spread out over a period of months rather than days, and again the level of official incompetence was very high. One eyewitness said: 'I was not only present at a sporting contest but also at a fair where there were sports, where there was cheating, where monsters were exhibited as a joke.'

The 1904 Games in St Louis, USA, were the last to be linked to an international fair.

Maybe the lowest point came during the 'Anthropology Days', when athletic contests ranging from pole-climbing to stone-throwing were arranged purely for 'savage peoples' including Africans, Patagonians and Sioux Indian tribesmen. Afterwards, one of the organizers concluded that 'the savage has been a very overrated man, from an athletic point of view'. Such an insulting and racist attitude to fellow human beings would not, of course, be tolerated today.

For a while after 1904, public interest was so low that it seemed there would be no more Games at all. Then in 1906 an **Interim** Games was held in Athens, in an attempt to get back to the spirit and success of 1896. In this, they very largely succeeded – thus whetting the world's appetite for the next official Games: in London in 1908. But London would have its own troubles....

Do you need assistance?

The London Games of 1908 were quite well organized but there was plenty of arguing too. The competitions themselves were all run by the British. This led to protests from the French, Canadians, Italians and Swedes about official rulings. But the most bitter opposition came from representatives of the USA – especially over the twice-run 400 metres final which ended up featuring only one athlete: a Briton. Afterwards the International Olympic Committee gave the control and judging of individual competitions to the international federation that governed each sport. The story of what happened in the marathon shows why this was a good idea....

The man with ideal legs

The marathon took place on 24 July – a hot, muggy day. The course began at Windsor Castle and ended at the Olympic stadium in Shepherd's Bush: 26 miles and 385 yards (or just over 42 kilometres) away. The 385 yards at the end were to be run around the stadium track, so that the finishing line was right in front of the **royal box**.

After 20 miles it seemed like a two-horse race for the gold. The leader was South African Charles Hefferon but closing fast was a small short-legged Italian from Carpi.

Dorando Pietri is illegally helped over the finishing line of the marathon at the 1908 London Olympics.

The Italian's name was Dorando Pietri. When asked if the shortness of his legs was a problem for a marathon runner, he said that they were ideal since they were 'exactly long enough to reach from the hips to the ground'!

Everybody loves you when you're down and out

The crowd lining the route now took a big hand in events. Hefferon, tiring, accepted a glass of champagne from someone two miles from the stadium. Not a good idea. He soon had stomach cramps and grew dizzy. Well-wishers then urged on Pietri so keenly that he upped his pace too far from the finish.

The spectators inside the stadium thus saw the little Italian appear first. He had only 385 yards to go. But in his exhaustion he was running the wrong way! The track officials rushed to set him right, then he collapsed. What should the officials and doctors do – just leave him there or run to his aid? If he was helped he would surely be disqualified. They decided to get him back to his feet. On Pietri kept plodding, down he kept falling, up his helpers kept rushing. But now a second runner entered the stadium. Not Hefferon from South Africa in the **British Empire** but *American* Bob Hayes! The race's head organizer Jack Andrews saw Hayes coming, he saw Pietri falling yet again – so he caught him and *carried* him across the line.

The Italian flag was hoisted up the victory pole even as Hayes crossed the line himself. Naturally the Americans made a furious protest. It was upheld, and while Pietri was stretchered away Hayes was declared the rightful winner – thus avoiding all-out war between the American camp and the British officials! The next day Pietri, fully recovered, claimed that he would have won without help. Queen Alexandra presented him with a **consolation** gold cup. And although the little man from Carpi had no medal to take home, news of his run soon made him more famous than many a true Olympic champion.

What is a professional?

The 1912 Olympics in Stockholm have been called 'the Harmonious Games'. Unlike the previous Games in St Louis, Paris and London, they were well organized and well reported, and they passed off without any major problems – at the time. But a year later, a news story broke about one of the athletes who had taken part. One of the biggest Olympic controversies was about to blow up.

'Bright Path''s road to fame

Jim Thorpe was born in 1888, to parents of mixed Native American, French and Irish blood. His mother gave him the Indian name Wa-tho-huck: 'Bright Path'. Jim first won national fame as an American-football player. A true all-rounder, he even won the 1912 **inter-collegiate** ballroom dancing championship! In that year, he was also chosen as a member of the American Olympic team. As befitted so **versatile** an athlete, his events were to be the **track-and-field pentathlon** (long jump, javelin, discus, 200 metres, 1500 metres) and the **decathlon** (long jump, javelin, discus, 1500 metres, high jump, pole vault, shot-put, 110 metres hurdles, 100 metres, 400 metres).

Thorpe won gold medals in both events. Not only that, he was also presented with a jewel-encrusted cup by the Tsar of Russia. Then King Gustav V of Sweden gave him a bronze **bust** for winning the pentathlon. 'Sir,' he said to Thorpe on handing it over, 'you are the greatest athlete in the world.' And what did the shy Thorpe reply? 'Thanks, King'! Thorpe returned to lead a **ticker-tape parade** in New York City.

Jim Thorpe had never competed in a decathlon before winning the gold medal at the 1912 Olympics. His performance was so good that it would have won him a silver medal at the 1948 Games.

10

In 1931 Thorpe sold the film rights to his life for $1500. 20 years later, a film based on his life was released, starring Burt Lancaster.

'Rules are like steamrollers'

In 1913 a reporter discovered that, years earlier, Thorpe had briefly earned $25 a week playing minor-league baseball. The amount of money was tiny, but technically it made Thorpe a **professional** sportsman – and all Olympic competitors in those days were meant to be **amateurs**. Thorpe protested that he had not even known about the amateur rule back then. He also pointed out that since his Olympic triumph, he had turned down offers of *thousands* of dollars to profit from his talents.

It did no good. His medals were taken back and his feats were wiped out of the Olympic record books. 'Rules are like steamrollers,' Thorpe wrote later. 'There is nothing they won't do to flatten the man who stands in their way.' Thorpe's own life went rather flat afterwards. After playing baseball and American football for a while, he became a drifter and died of a heart attack in 1953.

Most ordinary people felt that Thorpe had been treated very harshly. The people of Mauch Chunk in Pennsylvania, where he was buried, actually changed their small town's name to 'Jim Thorpe'. And in 1951, a sportswriters' poll voted him the greatest athlete of the first half of the century. In 1943 his supporters began to request the **reinstatement** of his medals and records. It turned out to be a very long campaign but finally it met with success. In 1982 the International Olympic Committee agreed to lift the ban on Jim Thorpe. His name was written back into the Olympic roll of fame and in 1983 his gold medals were re-presented to his children.

Racing against racism

The International Olympic Committee (IOC) decides where each Olympic Games is to be held. It takes its decision several years in advance. Then the host city has plenty of time to make all the necessary preparations. In 1931 the IOC decided that the 1936 Games would be held in Berlin, the capital of Germany. The Germans were one of the world's leading sporting nations, and they could be relied on to organize a successful Olympics. But then in 1933, something unforeseen happened. A new political party was elected to power in Germany. Its name was the National Socialist German Workers' Party – **Nazi** for short – and its leader was Adolf Hitler.

Olympic spirit or Olympic spite?

Soon people inside and beyond Germany learned that Hitler and his followers held racist views. These included the belief that white-skinned, 'racially pure' Germans were superior in all ways to other peoples, particularly Jews or blacks. Signs with messages like 'Dogs and Jews are not allowed' appeared in Germany. The Nuremberg Laws of 1935 declared Jews to be 'subhuman'. It became clear that Hitler wanted to use the Berlin Games of August 1936 as a **showcase** for his idea of the German 'Super Race'.

Jewish communities outside Germany called for a **boycott** of the Games. In the USA there was an especially strong campaign. But the Nazis assured the IOC that they would abide by the rules of Olympic competition. Two 'half-Jews' were even selected for the German national team. So the Games went ahead as planned.

The official poster for the 1936 Olympics.

GERMANY
BERLIN·1936
1ᵇ-16ᵇ AUGUST

OLYMPIC GAMES

Triumph of the 'black mercenaries'

Before 1936 Germany had not excelled in **track and field** events. But early in the Berlin Games, policeman Hans Woellke became the first German track-and-field gold medallist ever – in the shot-put. Hitler and his supporters were delighted. But their joy was not going to last.

Jesse Owens in action. Four years after his death in 1980, a Berlin street was renamed after him – a fitting tribute to one of the greatest Olympians of all.

The USA ended up with 25 medals in track and field – and thirteen were won by African-Americans, whom the Nazis called 'black **mercenaries**'. One of these supreme black athletes was Jesse Owens, gold medallist in the 100 metres, 200 metres, long jump and 4 × 100 metres relay. In spite of all the Nazi **propaganda**, the German people made Owens the hero of the Games. They even thrust autograph books through his Olympic-village bedroom window while he was trying to get some sleep!

There is a story that after Owens won the 100 metres final, a furious Hitler refused to meet him – even though he had congratulated other gold medallists. This may or may not be true. What *is* true is that when Owens went home to the USA, American President Franklin D Roosevelt failed to invite him to the White House. He did not even send him a letter of praise on his awesome Olympic feats. Thanks to racial laws in the USA Owens, like other black people, was not seen as equal to his white fellow-Americans. His Olympic brilliance gave a huge boost to the pride of African-Americans. But even 32 years later, long after Hitler and his hateful ideas had disappeared, true racial equality had still not been achieved in the USA (see next page).

Podium protests

The 1968 Games in Mexico City were controversial even before they began. The Olympics had never been held at such **altitude** before – over 2000 metres above sea level. Many experts feared that athletes unused to the very thin air might die from pushing themselves too hard. These were also the Games in which sex-tests were to be introduced. (This was because some women were suspected of chemically 'improving' their bodies with human growth hormones, thus making themselves – technically – men!)

And then, ten days before the Games were due to begin, Mexico City became the scene of a bloodbath when the Mexican army opened fire on a big student **demonstration**. About 260 people were killed and around 1200 injured. Shock waves from this were felt all around the sporting world. But the International Olympic Committee called it an 'internal affair' which was 'under control'. The Games could still go on – under their official slogan: 'Everything is possible with peace.'

'American' or 'Negro'?

Once the Games began, the biggest debate came after the 200 metres final for men. Black American Tommie Smith cruised home in a new world-record time of 19.83 seconds. In third place was fellow-black-American John Carlos, the previous-world-record holder. Both men belonged to the Olympic Project for Human Rights – a group of athletes who campaigned for better treatment for blacks in the USA – and they wanted the world to know about racial **inequality** there.

Tommie Smith and John Carlos make their peaceful protest on the podium in Mexico City, 1968. When Carlos was accused of 'tainting' the Games by making a political point, he said the Olympics were already highly political. 'Why do they play national anthems? ...' he asked. 'Why can't everyone wear the same colours but wear numbers to tell them apart? What happened to the Olympic ideal of man against man?'

So when they stepped up on to the podium to collect their medals, they went barefoot. And when the American anthem played, they both bowed their heads and raised a black-gloved hand in a 'Black Power' salute.

They explained later that their bare feet were a reminder of black American poverty, and their clenched fists showed black strength and unity. 'White America will only give us credit for an Olympic victory,' said Carlos. 'They'll say I'm an American, but if I did something bad, they'd say I was a Negro.' In the eyes of the US Olympic Committee, this protest was something bad. Both men were quickly banned from the team and ordered out of the Olympic village. Back at home, they then found it hard to make a living for many years. But they had drawn the world's attention to a very big problem – and in a completely peaceful way.

Flashback to 1936

At the Berlin Games of 1936 the marathon was won in style by Korean athlete Sohn Kee-Chung. Fellow-Korean Nam Seung-Yang picked up the bronze. But at that time their homeland was being **occupied** by Japan. So they were forced to run in the colours of Japan, and they even had to take Japanese names. To show their dissatisfaction, after receiving their medals they bowed their heads in silent protest while the Japanese national anthem was played.

In later years Sohn was able to enjoy the Games a little more. At the opening ceremony in 1948 he carried the flag of a now-free South Korea. And in 1988 in Seoul, South Korea's capital, he carried the Olympic torch into the stadium, at the age of 76.

The USA's gold-medal-winning 4 × 400 m team leaves the arena in Mexico City with a clenched-fist salute, showing solidarity with their fellow African-Americans.

Black September

The 1972 Games were held in Munich, West Germany. No expense was spared in staging the biggest Olympics ever. The last time the Games had taken place on German soil – in 1936 – Adolf Hitler's ruling **Nazi** Party had tried to undermine the true Olympic spirit (see pages 12 and 13). There was to be none of that in 1972 – at least not from the organizers. And just before the opening, to make sure that 27 African nations did not carry out their threat to **boycott** the Games, the International Olympic Committee (IOC) expelled Rhodesia for its policy of **white supremacy**.

It now seemed that little could go wrong. In purely sporting terms, very little did. With over 4000 representatives of the world's **media** present, records tumbled as never before. But the Games' sheer size, and the interest they created all over the world, also attracted to Munich people with *no* interest in sport. On the morning of 5 September they made their presence felt.

Worst-case scenario

The Munich Games were meant to be really friendly. As a result, security was quite minimal. That was how eight Palestinian Arab **terrorists** managed to get into the Olympic Village. Ever since 1948, Arabs and Israelis had been at odds with each other in the Middle East. On 5 September 1972 the Arabs headed for the Israeli quarters, killed two people there and took nine more as **hostages**.

On 6 September 1972, 84,000 people filled the Olympic stadium in Munich to remember those who had died in the Olympic Games' worst act of terrorism.

They now demanded the release of 200 Arab prisoners from Israeli jails – as well as a safe passage to Egypt for themselves. After long negotiations, the terrorists and their hostages were allowed to go to the military airport. There, West German marksmen killed three of the terrorists. But a gun battle followed, in which all nine Israeli hostages were killed, along with two more Arabs and a policeman. After such an awful tragedy what could happen next?

'The Games must go on'

The next morning, the Games were suspended for a memorial service in a packed Olympic stadium. Some people felt that the Games should now be declared over – and a few athletes left Munich for fear of another terrorist outrage. But finally the IOC decided to continue with the programme.

The aim of the terrorists had been to disrupt the Games, argued IOC President Avery Brundage, so why should they get what they wanted? Besides, if *they* managed to stop the Olympics in its tracks, how many other similar groups might try to do the same in future? The Israeli officials were in full agreement with this. The Games went on with their blessing. And since that dreadful day in 1972, terrorism has not been a major Olympic issue – but providing tight security *has* been.

After the tragedy, the 1972 Games continued – but lesser controversies continued to occur. Despite his lunge for the line in the 800 m final, Russian Evgeni Arzhanov lost to American Dave Wottle (in the cap) by 0.03 seconds. Wottle was so shocked at winning that he forgot to take off his cap during the national anthem – people thought he was making a protest of some kind.

Misery in Montreal

Sporting achievements took most of the headlines at the 1976 Games in Montreal, Canada, but in financial terms they could hardly have been more disastrous. For a variety of reasons, the cost of staging the Olympics in 1976 was 60 per cent higher than the cost of staging them in Munich four years earlier. When the Games finished, the **taxpayers** of Montreal had to pay off a **deficit** of $1 billion. It took them until 1996 – just before the Atlanta Games – to do this. Yet Mayor Jean Drapeau had claimed 'the Games could no more produce a deficit than a man could have a baby'!

All Blacks bring the blues

Once the Games got under way, there were around 1000 fewer competitors than in Munich. This was because more than 30 countries were either banned or refused to take part. As in 1971, Rhodesia was banned because blacks and whites were still kept separate due to that country's system of **white supremacy**. The island of Taiwan withdrew because the Canadian Government refused to recognize it as the Republic of China – a title that it disputed with mainland, **Communist**, China. But by far the largest number of absentee nations came from Africa. Their reason for staying away was all tied up with rugby union – not even an Olympic sport.

When the 1976 Games opened in Montreal, work on the Olympic facilities was still going on. This was due partly to bad weather conditions during the long winter, partly to workers' strikes and partly to a serious lack of funds. But the *Montreal Star* newspaper pointed out that the organizers took some strange decisions.

For example 33 cranes were hired by the constructors of the Olympic stadium at a cost of $1 million – and then some of them were never even used!. It would have been cheaper to have bought the cranes outright A much tighter security operation, after what had happened at the Munich Games, also contributed to the vast expense.

The awesome New Zealand rugby team is called the All Blacks (after the colour of their kit). These All Blacks had recently made a tour of South Africa which, like Rhodesia, was banned from the Olympics on account of its **apartheid** policy. Over 20 African nations, plus Guyana and Iraq, now demanded that the International Olympic Committee (IOC) should ban New Zealand from the 1976 Olympics. When the IOC refused, the protesting nations, led by Tanzania, took their own action by **boycotting** the Games – which were all the poorer for their absence.

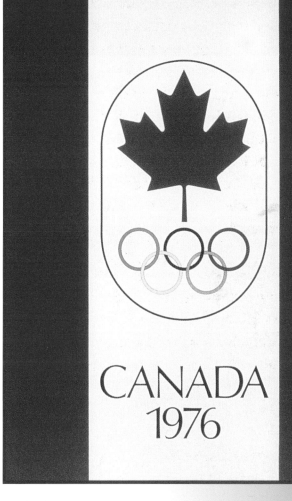

The official poster for the 1976 Games in Montreal, which have gone down in Olympic history as a financial fiasco.

Burning of the boat

In spite of all these troubles, the Montreal Olympics were still hugely enjoyable to watch and take part in. Triple-gold medallist Nadia Comaneci, a fourteen-year-old Romanian gymnast, became a popular symbol of all that was *right* about the Games. Even so, not everyone was happy. Two British yachtsmen, Allen Warren and David Hunt, finished fourteenth out of sixteen entries in the Tempest class. After the final race, they calmly set their boat on fire then waded ashore to watch it burn! 'I tried to persuade my skipper [Warren] to burn with the ship,' joked Hunt, 'but he wouldn't agree.'

The last disappointment came for the poor Canadians themselves. The final medal table showed not a single gold for the host country – the first time that had ever happened at the Summer Games!

Medal muddle

Article 46 of the Olympic rules clearly states that 'the Olympic Games are not competitions between nations'. It has not always seemed that way. Until 1908 athletes entered the Games as individuals, not as chosen members of a national team. That was the original Olympic ideal. Since then, however, one of the most popular features of any Games has been the medals table.

The International Olympic Committee still does not officially recognize national medal totals. But for the **media** and the public, they are often too fascinating to ignore. After all, how else can you tell at a glance which country is 'winning' the Games?

Who are the champions?

The two tables show the final medals totals at the 1928 Games in Amsterdam and then at the 1976 Games in Montreal. In 1928 all the leading nations came from Europe and North America. By 1976 that had changed, with Cuba, Japan and the part-Asiatic **USSR** making appearances.

In that year, all top ten nations were under **Communist** rule except for the USA, West Germany and Japan. Throughout the **Cold War** period, many Communist governments sponsored sport very heavily – and reaped the reward in Olympic gold medals.

NATIONAL MEDAL TOTALS, 1928 AND 1976

Amsterdam 1928

	G	S	B
USA	22	18	16
Germany	10	7	14
Finland	8	8	9
Sweden	7	6	12
Italy	7	5	7
Switzerland	7	4	4
France	6	10	5
Netherlands	6	9	4
Hungary	4	5	0
Canada	4	4	7

Montreal 1976

	G	S	B
USSR	49	41	35
East Germany	40	25	25
USA	34	35	25
West Germany	10	12	17
Japan	9	6	10
Poland	7	6	13
Bulgaria	6	9	7
Cuba	6	4	3
Romania	4	9	14
Hungary	4	5	13

A nation's position in the medals table is determined by its gold-medal count. If a nation has no gold medals, it is ranked according to its silver or its bronze count.

Valeri Borzov of the USSR wins the 200 m gold at the 1972 Games. He refused to give an interview after the race because, he said, American journalists had insulted him after he won the 100 m final.

According to one East German official at Montreal in 1976, this 'proved the success of our socialist (Communist) system and our training methods'. In Western countries like the USA and West Germany, governments did not usually get so directly involved, but were just as keen to see their athletes do well. In a way, the struggle to win gold became a kind of sporting warfare.

Basketball battle

Some athletes were dismayed by this international rivalry – especially between the USA and the USSR. Montreal champion swimmer John Naber said: 'Gold medals don't mean the White House is better than the **Kremlin**. It means I swam faster than anyone else, that's all.' But few could doubt that more than mere sport was at stake in Munich in 1972, when the USA took on the USSR in the Games' final basketball match.

Ever since 1936, when the sport first figured at the Games, the USA had never lost a game. And when the horn sounded for the end of this one, they were ahead by 50 points to 49. But the Brazilian referee overruled the clock. The game was briefly restarted, then the horn sounded again. Now a higher official ruled that, thanks to an earlier mix-up, three more seconds should be added on. The USSR team pulled off a court-long move which ended with a basket. And amid enormous uproar, they were given the victory by 51 points to 50. The US team, disgusted at having been 'cheated', refused to accept their silver medals. To lose any Olympic match was bad enough. But to lose to the USSR – and in such controversial circumstances – *that* was almost unbearable.

The USA had never lost a basketball match at the Olympics before 1972. In 1988, they had to settle for the bronze medal as two Communist nations, the USSR and Yugoslavia, played each other in the final.

Politics stopped play

'In ancient days,' one-time International Olympic Committee (IOC) President Avery Brundage once said, 'nations stopped wars to compete in the Games. Nowadays we stop the Olympics to continue our wars.' Political conflict certainly had an impact on the Games in 1980.

The Nearly Man

David Wallechinsky described in his brilliant *Complete Book of the Olympics* how the various boycotts of the 1970s and 1980s affected one unlucky individual. Bruce Kennedy was an excellent javelin-thrower from Rhodesia. In 1972, he was selected for the Rhodesian team to travel to Munich. But the IOC banned Rhodesia from taking part because of the racist system of government in that country.

He was selected again for Montreal in 1976, but Rhodesia was still excluded. Then, by marrying an American citizen, he qualified for the USA team which would go to Moscow in 1980. That team, of course, never arrived in the USSR thanks to the boycott over the invasion of Afghanistan. By then, though, Rhodesia (renamed Zimbabwe) had been allowed back into the Olympic fold.

In 1984 Kennedy was absolutely determined to get into an Olympic stadium. And at last he managed it — as an usher!

US President Jimmy Carter was the man behind the boycott of the 1980 Games in Moscow.

No go for Moscow

Political rivalry between the USA and the **USSR** had figured in most Games since 1952. It came to a head at the 1980 Olympics – and threatened to wreck the Olympic Movement altogether. These Games were due to be held in Moscow, the capital city of the **Communist**-ruled USSR (otherwise known as the Soviet Union). In 1979, Soviet forces had invaded Afghanistan – and US President Jimmy Carter responded with a call to **boycott** the 1980 Games. As a result, an almighty controversy broke out.

A Dutch member of the IOC said it was 'unjust to make athletes the conscience of the world'. Each National Olympic Committee had to decide what to do. Rule 26 of the Olympic Charter says that the Committees 'must be **autonomous** and must resist all pressure of any kind whatsoever, whether of a political, religious or economic nature'. Some governments friendly to the USA, like Britain and Australia, backed the boycott but said their athletes could choose for themselves whether to travel to Moscow. That was not quite so easy for American athletes – President Carter threatened to **revoke** the passport of any competitor who tried to get to the USSR.

In the end only 80 nations took part in the Moscow Games (in 1984 there would be 140). But more world records were set than in 1976, and there were plenty of supremely memorable contests. But many fans believed the Games were 'devalued' by the absence of the USA, West Germany, China, Japan and many other great sporting nations in the biggest Olympic boycott yet.

In 1980 Alan Wells (left) became only the second Briton to win the 100 m at the Olympic Games. American athletes, who were absent from Moscow, had won twelve of the previous nineteen contests.

The Russians aren't coming – but Zola Budd is!

After the American-led **boycott** of the 1980 Games in the **USSR**, it was the USA's turn to stage the 1984 Games. And guess what? The USSR organized its own fourteen-nation boycott! The Soviet authorities refused to let their athletes attend partly as a protest over **'commercialization'** (see picture below) and partly due to doubts about the level of security in Los Angeles. It seemed clear to many, however, that this was a simple act of revenge for the 1980 boycott.

Collision course

A new event was due to appear in the **track-and-field** programme at Los Angeles: the 3000 metres for women. Two runners with very different backgrounds were determined to take part in it: Mary Decker of the USA and South African Zola Budd. Decker had been an infant **prodigy**. At the age of twelve, she ran a marathon in just over three hours, a 440 metres, an 880 metres, a mile race then a two-mile race – all in the space of one week! But around the age of fifteen all the running badly affected her growing body, and she missed the 1976 Games through illness. By 1980, however, she was back with a vengeance: setting a world record for the mile, and raring to take on the world's best in the Moscow Games of 1980. The boycott shattered that dream, but it only made her more determined to run in Los Angeles – her home town – in 1984.

British **decathlon** gold-medallist Daley Thompson models an interesting T-shirt in Los Angeles. The back of the shirt criticized the broadcasts of the ABC television network, which focused closely on American winners at the expense of other nations.

ABC had paid $225 million for exclusive TV transmission rights – a massive step up from the $394,000 fee paid by CBS in 1960. In the eyes of some, this led to an unacceptable commercialization of the Games.

Zola Budd's home town was Bloemfontein, South Africa. She had a poster of her heroine, Decker, on her bedroom wall. But by 1983, aged seventeen and running barefoot, she was ranked number one in the world at 5000 metres. And in January 1984, she broke Decker's world record at that distance by six seconds. But to get to Los Angeles, Budd had to change her nationality. As a South African, she was barred from competing (see page 19). So she moved to Britain, her grandfather's homeland, became a British citizen instead, and got into the *British* team.

Decker on the deck

Thus the stage was set for a great Decker–Budd showdown in Los Angeles. It turned out to be one of the most controversial races ever. After 1700 metres Budd led, followed closely by Decker. What happened next depended on whose side you took. Budd and Decker got into a tangle, and Budd was briefly thrown off balance. Five strides later, it happened again. Decker tripped over Budd's leg, cutting the barefoot leader's heel with her spikes. Decker fell awkwardly and was out of the race in agony.

Budd ran on – bleeding from the clash, and soon crying too because Decker's home crowd of over 85,000 was booing her so loudly. She came in seventh, and was then disqualified for 'causing' Decker's downfall. Later, that decision was overruled, but a huge dispute blew up between the American and British **media** over who had been at fault. In the end, almost everyone agreed that it had been an unfortunate accident. But neither woman was destined to win any medal at all at future Games.

Budd (151) vs Decker (373). Many events in 1984 were scheduled at American TV's main viewing time, even though this was the middle of the night in Europe.

Failing the test

For many people, the men's 100 metres sprint is *the* big Olympic event. As the athletes lined up for the 100 metres final at Seoul in 1988, the world held its breath. In under ten seconds, the World's Fastest Man would be revealed. Carl Lewis, the 1984 champion, was running. So was world-record holder Ben Johnson from Canada. They had not always got on well. Lewis suspected that Johnson took illegal drugs called steroids to 'improve' his performance. Just 9.79 seconds later, Johnson thrust his arm in the air to smash his own world record. Second-placed Lewis was surer than ever that Johnson had cheated. And at the post-race drug test, he was proved right.

Passing the test!

At the 1968 Games in Mexico, British bricklayer Chris Finnegan won the middleweight boxing crown. He could barely describe his feelings: 'the nearest I've felt to it was when walking down the aisle with my old woman after our wedding ... only there was no gold medal at the end of that!' But then he had to perform again – by giving a urine sample that could be tested for drugs. To everyone's frustration, it took him until 1.40 the next morning (and several pints of beer) before he could provide the sample – then pass the test.

'I know what it's like to cheat'

Drug-testing of urine samples was introduced at the 1968 Olympics. Since then 42 athletes had been disqualified – and disgraced – for failing their tests. Ben Johnson was the 43rd but no star so famous had been caught before.

Ben Johnson of Canada won the Seoul 100 m final in 1988 by a margin that was just too big to be true.

Shock waves from Seoul rippled all over the world. And it got worse. Later enquiries showed that Johnson had been taking steroids since 1981 – plus growth hormones which were taken from human corpses! In 1989 Johnson publicly confessed and pleaded with young athletes not to follow his example. 'It happened to me,' he said in tears. 'I've been there. I know what it's like to cheat.'

All in the blood

Finland's Lasse Viren won the 5000 m and 10,000 m at both the 1972 and 1976 Games. Although no one could prove it, some suspected him of 'blood doping' to achieve his great Olympic feats. This technique, which was not then illegal, involved taking out some of an athlete's blood, storing it for a week or two, then re-injecting it just before a big race. This would improve the body's intake of oxygen.

Viren always laughed at the suspicions, and said he trained 'on reindeer milk'. But in 1984, fellow-Finn Martti Vainio lost his 10,000 m silver medal when traces of a steroid were found in his sample. It is believed that he stopped *taking* steroids three weeks before the race – hoping not to be caught – but thanks to blood doping, steroids were brought back into his bloodstream.

Super-sprinter Florence Griffith Joyner of the USA won three gold medals at Seoul. Some people suspected 'Flojo' of using drugs to achieve phenomenal times after an unspectacular start to her career. She passed every drug test she took, but retired in 1989 just before *random* (unannounced) testing came in.

Sadly she died of a heart seizure in 1998, aged only 38. People who still suspected her pointed out that steroid use can lead, in the long term, to an overloading of the heart and damage to the **arteries**. One of the sad effects of drugtaking in sport is that *any* amazing feat immediately seems suspicious, even if the sportsman or woman is completely innocent.

From Atlanta to Australia

Terrorist attacks have been mercifully rare at the modern Olympic Games. Since the tragedy at Munich in 1972 (see pages 16 and 17), each host city has made security a top priority. But at the **Centennial** Games in Atlanta in 1996, terrorism reared its grotesque head again.

On Day Nine of the Games, a crude pipe bomb exploded inside the Centennial Olympic Park. This was a nine-hectare area of corporate tents where sports fans from all over the world could meet and enjoy the Olympic atmosphere. The bomb killed two of them and wounded about 100 more.

Atlanta had advertised itself as 'a city too busy to hate'. Clearly, that was not absolutely true. But three days after the bombing, the Park reopened and the fans flocked back. Like the Munich Games in 1972, the show had to go on – in spite of this sick and cowardly attempt to disrupt it.

Mr. Ivester   Mr. Goizueta   Mr. Samaranch   Mr. Pound

The Coca-Cola Company, which has its headquarters in Atlanta, was closely involved in the bidding for the 1996 Olympics. Billy Payne, an ex-football player who played a major part in bringing the Games to Atlanta, said, 'I figured most good things that get done in this community have very much a history of being supported by the Coca-Cola Company.'

The Company finally spent around $200 million on Olympic sponsorship, advertising, promotion and hospitality. This led some to refer to the 1996 Olympics as the 'Coke Games'. But the Coca-Cola connection will not end in Atlanta. As one International Olympic Committee vice-president put it, 'No matter where the Games are, Coca-Cola will be there.'

On to Sydney, 2000

The Games of the year 2000 are due to be held in Sydney, Australia. The last time Australia staged the Games was in 1956, when Melbourne was host city. That was in the middle of the **Cold War**. Holland, Switzerland and Spain **boycotted** the Games in a protest against the **USSR's** brutal treatment of a rising in Hungary. Egypt, Lebanon and Iraq also withdrew in protest at the Israeli-led takeover of the Suez Canal. Further difficulties were caused by Australia's location, which – in those days – made it difficult and expensive for many of the world's best athletes to get there.

Getting to Sydney in 2000 should not be too great a problem. Quite apart from the 10,000-plus competitors who are expected to take part, spectators from overseas will probably number well over a million. What they will witness at the Millennium Olympics cannot be predicted. But if previous Games are anything to go by, there will almost certainly be some kind of controversy!

Just as in earlier Games held in the USA, there were murmurings of discontent in Atlanta about local 'favouritism'.

The brilliant American runner Michael Johnson wanted to become the first man in history to win both the 200 m and the 400 m. But thanks to the sequence of events on the track, it was not possible for him to make the attempt. Amid some controversy, the organizers decided to alter the programme to let Johnson take part in both events.

In due course this extraordinary athlete won double-gold, and set a phenomenally fast, new world-record time of 19.32 secs in the 200 m.

Glossary

altitude height above sea level

amateur someone who competes for fun, rather than as a job, and who is unpaid

apartheid policy of keeping black people apart from, and inferior to, whites

artery part of the human body which helps to convey blood from the heart

autonomous self-governing, free from outside interference

boycott to refuse to have anything to do with a person, country or event

British Empire collection of countries around the world once ruled by Britain

bust sculpture of a person's head, shoulders and chest

centennial the hundredth anniversary of something

Cold War period, after World War Two, of unfriendly relations between the USA and the USSR, which never became real warfare

commercialization attempt to make money from something

Communism the idea that a single ruling political party can provide for all its people better than if they are left to make their own decisions and keep their own homes, land and businesses. The USSR became the first Communist state in 1917. After World War Two, the USSR introduced Communism into much of eastern Europe.

consolation a prize given not for winning, but for just missing out

decathlon competition containing ten different events: 100 metres, 110 metres hurdles, 400 metres, 1500 metres, high jump, long jump, pole vault, javelin, discus and shot-put

deficit amount by which a sum of money is too small. For example, if someone needs £5 and has £1, there is a deficit of £4.

demonstration public protest about an issue

hostage someone who is held as a prisoner until certain demands are met

inequality lack of fairness between different groups in society

inter-collegiate competition between different colleges

interim taking place in between official Games

Kremlin headquarters of the government of the USSR

media plural of medium (of communication), for example newspapers, magazines, TV and radio

mercenary person who is purely working for pay or other rewards

Nazi short form of the National Socialist German Workers' Party, a political party led by Adolf Hitler

occupied invaded and held by force

pentathlon competition containing five different events

pervert undermine or abuse

prodigy someone, especially a child, who is very talented

professional paid competitor

propaganda information put out to convince people of an idea or a view

reinstatement restoration

revoke take away

royal box special seats from which a royal family views public events

showcase acting as an advertisement for something

taxpayer person who pays a portion of their earnings to the government to pay for the running of the country

terrorist someone who uses violence to force a government to do what he or she wants

ticker-tape parade celebration where strips of paper are thrown to greet a hero or heroine

track and field sporting events which involve running, jumping, throwing and walking – such as the 100 metres or the javelin

USSR a Communist country, including Russia and many smaller nations, which broke up in 1991

versatile multi-talented or adaptable

white supremacy political arrangement or system of government by which white people, although small in numbers, have more rights and privileges than the black majority

Index